W9-BTC-156

IMAGES
of America
SPRING LAKE

In the tranquility of a secluded cove on the banks of Spring Lake, a pair of swans introduce their downy cygnets to the water with the dome of St. Catharine's Church in the background. (Mike Jones, photographer.)

Cover caption:
The essence of Spring Lake grandeur, with lofty turrets rising through the salt mist, was captured by G.W. Pach in this photograph looking south over the grounds of the eastern facade of Ballingarry. The Maloney Cottage on Morris Avenue has been placed on the National Register of Historic Places. (1903 G.W. Pach photograph, author's collection.)

Patricia F. Colrick

First published 1998

ISBN 0-7524-0583-7

Published by Arcadia Publishing,
an imprint of the Chalford Publishing Corporation,
One Washington Center, Dover, New Hampshire 03820.
Printed in Great Britain

Library of Congress Cataloging-in-Publication Data applied for

Mr. Johnson is at the reigns of a fringed surrey filled with friends ready for a drive through the unpaved streets of Spring Lake in this early 1900s photograph taken on Jersey Avenue by Nettie Megill. (Collection of Elizabeth P. Robinson.)

Contents

Acknowledgments

This book would not have been possible without the gracious cooperation of Mrs. Jeanne Duggan, whose extensive collection of Monmouth Hotel and other Spring Lake memorabilia forms the basis of this study; and Elizabeth P. Robinson, a granddaughter of Edward V. Patterson, the first mayor of Spring Lake Beach. Her interest in this project and enthusiasm for preserving what remains of historic Spring Lake has been an inspiration to me.

Others who have shared their extensive postcard and memorabilia collections with me are Dick Napolitan, Joseph A. Dunn, Robert Wohlforth, the late retired Police Chief Russell "Bunky" Hurden, and Jennie Lee Aitkenhead. The resources of the Monmouth County Archives were of inestimable value to this study, for it is there that the building contracts, tax records, and other documentation are being preserved for the benefit of the general public. I am most grateful to Mary Ann Kiernan, research assistant; and to Monmouth County Archivist Gary D. Saretzky and his entire staff for their dedicated professionalism. I am also grateful to Spring Lake Borough Clerk Maryann Coogan; Doris Billmeyer, librarian of the Free Public Library, Spring Lake; Louise Parr, librarian at the Wall Township Library; Charles D. Wrege, Ph.D., for his meticulous study of the Philadelphia Centennial and early Spring Lake; Joseph Benford, curator of the Print and Picture Collection of the Free Public Library of Philadelphia; Rev. Msgr. Joseph C. Shenrock, archivist for the Diocese of Trenton, whose book, *Upon This Rock*, documents the fascinating story of Catholicism in New Jersey; and Rev. Philip W. Zebley, for sharing his research on one of Spring Lake's founders, Dr. Alphonso Willits. I am also grateful to Gurney Lord, Msgr. Harrold Murray, Frank Heine, Mary Ann Kelly, Msgr. Thomas Leubking, historian Marie Sylvester, antiquarian book dealer and friend Richard Weiner, Col. Wesley Banse of Manasquan, Gilbert VanNote, columnist Mildred Colyard, photographers Mike Jones and Steve Lacko, historian George Moss, John Joseph Smith, Wick York, Maria Marucci, Carol Wallace, Eileen McLaughlin, and Robert Nesbitt. The landscape chapter was enhanced by the invaluable research information obtained from Catha Grace Rambusch of the *Catalogue of American Gardens* at Wave Hill, New York; Mary Daniels of Harvard University; Joyce Connolly of the Frederick Law Olmstead National Historic Site; Jodie Stock, University of California at Berkeley; and in Spring Lake, Roberta T. Schroeder and Lorelie Cheli. The Spring Lake Historical Society, located on the top floor of Borough Hall, maintains a wonderful display of Spring Lake memorabilia and study collections. It is a "must see" for anyone interested in the town and its history (call (732) 449-0772 for exhibiting hours). For additional reading, the Spring Lake Bicentennial's town history book by Dr. Charles D. Wrege and the Bicentennial History Committee is recommended, available at the museum. I am grateful to my editor, Jamie Carter, to Randall Gabrielan and Karen Schnitzsphan, both authors in this series, and to a friend and gifted instructor Bonnie DuBois for their enthusiastic encouragement. Lastly, my mother, Elizabeth E. Florio; sister Lisa; my husband, Edward; and our three children have been very helpful in many ways throughout this endeavor; they have allowed me to contribute the considerable time and dedication that the task required.

Introduction

Spring Lake is an oceanfront community bounded on the south by Wreck Pond, and on the north by Lake Como. It was named after a spring-fed body of water that was the locus of the first efforts of development that occurred in the 1870s. What existed for years as large farm tracts when present-day Spring Lake was part of greater Wall Township became in the 1870s sites for residential enclaves, most anchored by a hotel and with separate names, including Villa Park, Spring Lake Beach, Brighton, North Brighton, Como, and North Spring Lake—until their identities were subsumed under one town name.

Spring Lake's early period of development was spurred on by the introduction of rail service to the area. The closing of the nation's Centennial Exposition, held in Philadelphia from April to October of 1876, provided an opportunity for enterprising individuals to purchase and transport lumber and entire buildings to Spring Lake, where they were ingeniously reused for homes, hotels, and other structures. These substantially constructed "Centennial relics," as they came to be affectionately known, were obtained for considerably less than their original construction costs. Their movement was facilitated by the existing and expanding network of rail lines, while enjoying attendant publicity as well. As plans were being made for transporting Centennial buildings, a group of Philadelphians who laid out Spring Lake Beach included a hotel on its "ground plan" as a focal point that came to be known as the Monmouth House. As the popularity of the area increased, so too did the range of businesses as well as the number of private homes. Eventually, Monmouth Avenue and the lakefront became desirable locations for homes that were occupied seasonally, as well as shops to meet the needs of the largely summer inhabitants.

A study of the builders and designers of Spring Lake's remaining building stock reveals much of the values and tastes of that bygone era. Many accomplished architects, mainly based in Philadelphia, have designed private homes, hotels, and other institutions in Spring Lake. The sophistication of the clientele is evident in the artistry of the surviving churches, the impressive Memorial Community House, and the private estates. Once promoted as New Jersey's "garden spot," Spring Lake had several private landscape showplaces, as well as a tradition of maintaining superlative public grounds and its non-commercial boardwalk. The vested self-interest of the town's early developers in creating tasteful improvements has left enduring legacies to the community, many of which are explored in this book.

The photographic record for this elegant resort is equally as impressive as its architectural record. It was well documented in postcards, in postal novelty stamps, and in several large presentation albums created by G.W. Pach to impressively depict such showplaces like Ballingarry, the Casino, St. Catharine's and the Protestant Church, and the New Monmouth. Halves of stereographic sets included informal scenes on or around Spring Lake and the original Monmouth Hotel. When viewed through a stereoscope, complete with three-dimensional effect, the scenes effectively draw in the viewer—a powerful nineteenth-century advertising technique for an emerging resort. A unique glimpse into Spring Lake in the early part of the twentieth century is provided by the photo album, in Elizabeth P. Robinson's collection, of Miss Nettie Megill (1874–1946), a gifted amateur photographer. Her snapshots, mounted on black paper with white ink captions, record with simple eloquence the life in her hometown from about 1900 to 1912, when she worked in Mr. Potter's Third Avenue store.

Readers may notice the frequency with which Spring Lake's building stock was relocated. This is a practice that began with Centennial buildings and continued into the twentieth century. Even when "labor was cheap," developers and owners appreciated the value of well-built structures enough to move them, sometimes more than once, off their foundations and, using jacks, logs, and horses, relocate them to more desirable locations like so many monopoly pieces.

The study of a largely summertime community necessarily leads one to cast a wide net in research sources. The individuals who built their homes in Spring Lake and stayed for varying periods of time have left the town impressive and diverse structures. Although many of the important sites explored herein are no longer extant—the result of fires, demolition, changing tastes, and needs—enough remains to retain the special atmosphere that defines Spring Lake. It is present in the well-ordered streets of frame buildings, punctuated by turrets and welcoming porches. In presenting this chronologically arranged study of the buildings and builders of Spring Lake, I am hoping to broaden an appreciation for what has been built and to inspire those who seek to retain and restore the dream of historic Spring Lake.

One

Genesis of a Seaside Community

The proximity of a pristine, spring-fed lake to an ocean beach of soft sand inspired the early developers of Spring Lake, which remained part of greater Wall Township until the late nineteenth century.

The diminutive *c.* 1840s Georgian Revival farmhouse of farmer and U.S. Lifesaving Service Capt. Forman Osborn is thought to be the oldest house in Spring Lake. Its construction incorporates elements salvaged from area shipwrecks and its foundation stone is believed to be of English ship ballast. After Capt. Osborn sold his farm acreage to the Spring Lake Beach Improvement Company in 1875, Reverend Willits is said to have stayed at the farmhouse until his own house was built across the lake. (Courtesy of Dr. Charles D. Wrege.)

Reverend Willits's Passaic Avenue home of ample proportions was built on the northern side of the street opposite the lake and its perimeter park. Smith and Hughes of Germantown, Pennsylvania, were the carpenters, and it was depicted in the 1878 Woolman and Rose Atlas of Monmouth County. The three-story, gable-fronted home featured a mansard roof to maximize interior space. The addition of a gazebo-like porch wing further expanded the rambling porch. In 1913, this became the home of E.V. Patterson, former stationmaster, mayor, and businessman. (June P. Rounds, photographer.)

Rev. Alphonso A. Willits (1821–1913), the Philadelphia-based Presbyterian minister and lecturer, is credited with the discovery of Spring Lake's potential as a resort. He was known as "the apostle of sunshine," a metaphor that symbolized for him God's presence in all of creation. In the 1870s, he interested other prominent Philadelphians to purchase the Osborn farm acreage for summer cottages. He is said to have built the first cottage. (Collection of Elizabeth P. Robinson.)

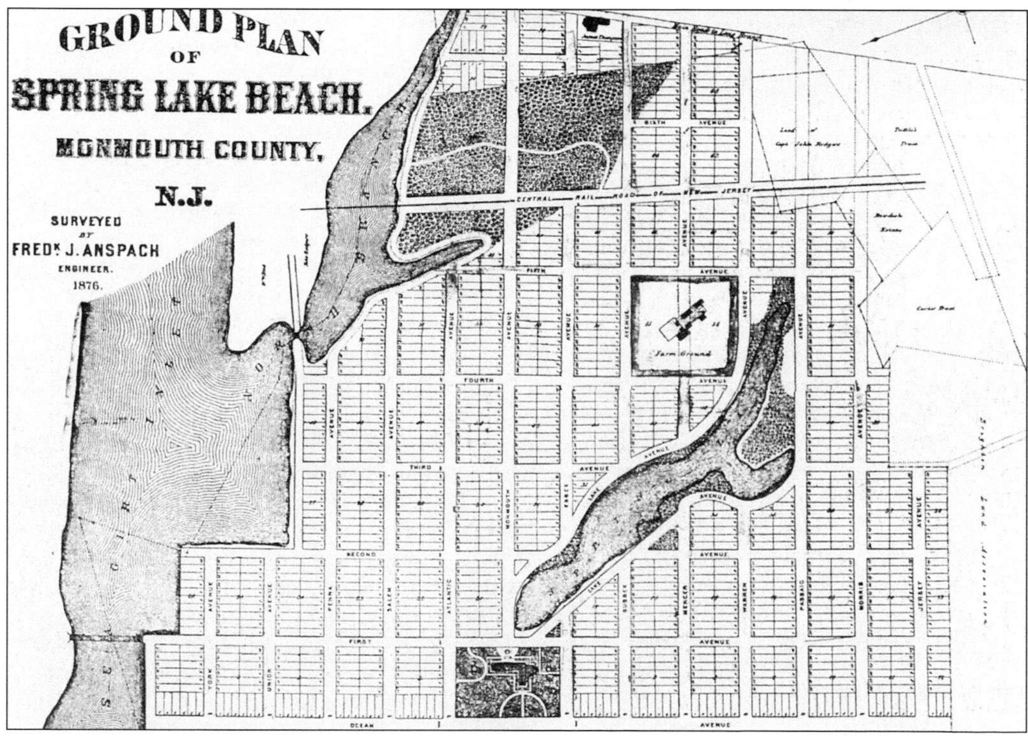

This map, entitled "Ground Plan of Spring Lake Beach" and dated 1876, was surveyed by Philadelphia engineer Frederick J. Anspach. Streets named after New Jersey counties were laid out in a grid pattern, through which the existing spring-fed body of water, "Spring Lake," cuts a diagonal path. Near the western edge of the lake was the railroad station and hotel, the Lake House. The other large hotel, the Monmouth House, had both ocean and lake frontage. (Map, Monmouth County Hall of Records.)

In November 1875, plans were drawn for a hotel that was to have both lake and ocean frontage. The Lake House Company engaged the services of W. Hotchkiss & Barber, of Williamsport, Pennsylvania, to build Spring Lake Beach's first major hotel, the Monmouth House, according to the plans of S.D. Button of Philadelphia. The structure had a 233-foot-wide frontage and was four stories high. From the time it opened on June 10, 1876, to its destruction by fire in 1900, the popularity it enjoyed fueled the growing interest in Spring Lake as a resort community. The following images were taken from a collection of stereoscopic views of the Monmouth House shortly before it opened and are in the collection of Mrs. Jeanne Duggan. The south entry of the hotel featured a wide stairway and circular driveway.

A circular parterre garden trimmed by roses was set at the Monmouth Avenue entrance to the Monmouth House at the foot of the lake. This style of landscape improvement, still carried on today in Spring Lake, is particularly impressive when viewed from above—and was surely enjoyed by hundreds of visitors who flocked to the ample hotel porches.

In this view looking southeast from one of the porches, sash-windows—high enough to step through—provided cooling breezes to the parlors of the main floor.

The well-appointed main office presented an efficient and elegant appearance.

This view down the hallway shows the elegant plaster consoles and 13-foot-high ceilings of the lobby. Newspaper accounts tell how, due to the popularity of the hotel, guests slept on cots in the halls at certain peak times.

In the lobby, an elaborate, tiered gas chandelier occupied the center of a parlor that featured delicate, cameo-back loveseats and armchairs reportedly shipped on rail cars from Grand Rapids.

Shiny urns and substantial worktables occupied the hotel's kitchen, which was set in an adjoining building to the north of the hotel measuring 56 by 95 feet.

Visitors take in the view from the east porch.

An octagonal, two-story-high pavilion with benches was built on a boardwalk between the Monmouth House and the ocean.

This tranquil scene of a sailboat near the beach was photographed from the elevated boardwalk pavilion.

This view shows the oceanfront bathhouses provided by the Monmouth House.

The view looking southwest from the Monmouth House shows the expanse of Wreck Pond in the distance. Tim Hurley's stables were at the corner of Atlantic and First Avenues.

CENTENNIAL

Department of Public Comfort.

(OFFICIAL.)

RECEPTION ROOM,

Opposite Main Entrance.

A convenient place, FREE OF CHARGE, where parties may meet on entering the Grounds, leave their Satchels, Baskets, Bundles, &c., and make arrangements for the day's pleasure.

THIS BUILDING CONTAINS

General Parlor,	Coat and Baggage Room,
Ladies' Parlor,	Barber Shop,
Ladies' Hair-Dressing,	Boot-Blacking Room,
Lavatories,	Theatre Ticket Office,

AND THE FAMOUS

"AMERICAN LUNCH COUNTER."

☞All charges are VERY MODERATE and under control of the CENTENNIAL BOARD OF MANAGERS.

The Public Comfort Building was removed from the Centennial Grounds and brought to Spring Lake, where it was reconstructed and modified to become the Lake House Hotel. (1876 Centennial guidebook view, courtesy of Mari and Chuck Slocum.)

The Lake House was removed and rebuilt by Smith & Hughes, who contracted with the painters Smith & Henry of Cape May to remove and reinstall the window glass throughout. The hotel, which opened in June 1877, was billed as a "family" place, with 92 rooms, fully carpeted , with large dining parlors on both its first and second floors, and "no bar." It had a bowling alley in a separate building and ran free coaches between the hotel and beach. It was demolished in 1904, replaced by a public park. This view shows the Lake Houseto the left, in the background, from the head of the lake. (Spring Lake Historical Society.)

The Centennial's Agricultural Hall, a 820-by-100-foot wide building with three transepts each 540 feet long, was purchased by an early area developer who sold one-half of it to Spring Lake Beach developers James and Thomas Hunter. Its lumber was used for eight homes, a station, and a 900-foot-long bridge over Wreck Pond Inlet connecting to Sea Girt, to the south. (Photograph from the Print and Picture Collection, Free Public Library of Philadelphia.)

This view shows the large scale of the Agricultural Hall during the Centennial, with an interior fountain in the foreground. (Photograph from the Print and Picture Collection, Free Public Library of Philadelphia.)

Spring Lake's first railroad depot, just west of the Lake House, is said to have been built from Centennial lumber. The variety in surface textures, including cedar siding, sawtooth shingles, and vertical siding in the attic story overhanging the gables and roof, gave the building a picturesque appeal. The stationmaster was Edward V. Patterson, Spring Lake Beach's first mayor, who lived there with his family until relocating to Monmouth Avenue in 1885. (Collection of Elizabeth P. Robinson.)

The Carleton House occupied three-quarters of the block west of the Monmouth House along First Avenue. The Queen Ann structure was the 1880 design of New York architect Bruce Price. Pictured here is a reproduction of the double-page spread featuring the same photographs from a 1895 railroad guidebook of Spring Lake.

The Patterson family sat for a formal portrait *c.* 1900. From left to right, they are (seated) Benjamin Y., Mary Annie Buckelew (Mrs. Patterson), Edward Vernou with baby Robert D., and Arden V.; (standing) Leon B., Edward V. Jr., and Mary Edna. Mr. Patterson, mayor from 1892 to 1903, purchased Reverend Chandler's Villa Park cottage and relocated it to Monmouth Avenue in 1885. After leaving the employ of the railroad, he formed a real estate and insurance business which moved from the railroad vicinity to Third Avenue. (Collection of Elizabeth P. Robinson.)

The Carlton Annex was designed in 1883 by Philadelphia architect Benjamin Linfoot to extend the popular hotel with rooms and ground floor stores. This second half of a 1895 view shows what a prominent location the intersection of Monmouth and First Avenues had become by the turn of the century. This commercial district was destroyed in the Monmouth Hotel fire of 1900. (Collection of Elizabeth P. Robinson.)

The seeds were planted for Third Avenue as a commercial district when Oliver Huff Brown (1852–1924) opened his home furnishing business at the northwest corner of Third and Jersey Avenues in 1882, expanding in 1884. The Getsinger Bros. did the brickwork and plastering, and John Middleton was the carpenter. Enlargements made in 1886 to the west and northern bay, with the artistic turret with porthole windows, expanded storage and showroom space. The furniture, floor coverings, china, and artful decorative effects catered primarily to the needs of "summer cottagers," expanding to include major hotels with a branch store in Lakewood. O.H. Brown, a mayor for 32 years, a state senator, banker, real estate investor, and philanthropist, was an individual who exerted an "impelling force" and influence upon Spring Lake. (Spring Lake Historical Society.)

The dry goods, real estate, and insurance store of William H. Potter, just to the north of O.H. Brown's store, opened in 1884. This local landmark, seen here *c.* 1904, was later J. Frank Cobb's and presently Town Shoppe, continuing a tradition of clothing and other essentials. The Spring Lake Directory of 1920 listed the shop's offerings: "straw hats, dress suit cases, outing shoes, bathing suits, men's outing shirts, tennis balls, and all summer requisites." (Nettie Megill, photographer.)

This unusual *c.* 1909 view captures a work scene looking west across Third Avenue from the Marucci Taylor Shop toward the English Tudor building designed for E.V. Patterson by Laurence Brazer in 1908. By 1910, Frank Marucci built an attractive two-story brick Classical Revival store and apartment building in this location. Frank Marucci was a councilman from 1916 until his election as mayor in 1936, serving until 1956. Marucci Park was named in his memory in 1959. (Collection of Maria Marucci.)

This substantially built building at the northeast corner of Third and Jersey Avenues, now a restaurant, was in the early 1890s the pharmacy of Daniel H. Hills, who also served as mayor of Spring Lake from 1924 to 1935. Pharmacist Charles Bye is to right in the photo, and next from the right is D.H. Hills in this *c.* 1890 photograph donated to the Borough by Ethel C. Fury.

Seen here in 1903, the First National Bank was organized in 1901 with O.H. Brown as president and other leaders in the business community on the executive board. The Classical Revival brick bank and post office building was a source of pride, and it continues to be the most imposing commercial structure in Spring Lake. (Photograph, G.W. Pach, Collection of Mrs. Jeanne Duggan.)

The year 1925 saw the last vacant lot vanish on Third Avenue, as Charles Lewis of Lewis Lumber Co. purchased property at the corner of Passaic and Third Avenues to build a substantial brick structure with shops below, adjacent to the 1910 Marucci building to the north. That year also saw the widening of Morris Avenue between Third and Fourth Avenues to provide additional parking for the shopping area. (1940s photograph, author's collection, gift of Mrs. Jeanne Duggan.)

Two

Three Grand Hotels

This 1950s aerial view of the southern tip of Spring Lake shows the heart of what became known as the hotel district. The Essex and Sussex is to the left of center in the foreground, along Ocean Avenue. (Collection of Mrs. Jeanne Duggan.)

Mrs. Anna W. Baird of Philadelphia, widow of Matthew Baird of Baldwin Locomotive, engaged Benjamin Linfoot to design a complex of seaside cottages on the block directly north of the Monmouth House in 1880, after purchasing the land from James Hunter. The block, bounded to the south and north by Essex and Sussex Avenues, was named "Hastings Square" after the historic port of Hastings, renown for its mild climate and fine sea-walk.

This "twin cottage" stood at Essex Avenue until 1992. This is a rendering of the original design by Linfoot from his *Summer Quarters* publication of 1882. (Courtesy of Atheneum of Philadelphia.)

Inset: Linfoot designed ten free-standing double cottages, each portion with its own entrance and with a unique but harmonious appearance along the perimeter of the Hastings Square quadrangle. Linfoot pointedly refrained from calling them Queen Ann, favoring instead American Cottages because of their porches and high basements. Here is the complex as seen from the dunes, *c.* 1900. (Nettie Megill, photographer.)

The Hastings Square complex was sold to the Hastings Square Hotel Company in 1914. The Philadelphia firm Guy King & Co. then designed the landmark Colonial Revival Essex and Sussex Hotel. In this view from an I. Taylor brochure, c. 1914, the oceanfront cottages are being prepared to be relocated to the north side of Essex Avenue. (Courtesy of Marie Sylvester.)

The colossal columns of the main porch of the Essex and Sussex created a shaded and comfortable area for relaxing, as seen in this late-1940s photo. (Collection of Mrs. Jeanne Duggan.)

The dining room, gracious ballroom, and more casual cocktail lounge were featured in a 1930s hotel brochure.

An enchanting courtyard with a rose-covered pergola and swimming pool looked out on the lake to the west.

Colossal paired columns denote the main entry of the hotel in this late-1920s view, which also illustrates the impressive view from the hotel's upper floors.

The well-appointed main lobby of the hotel featured Edwardian furnishings supplied by O.H. Brown, a stockholder in the hotel by 1914. Propriety dictated that guests returning from the beach were provided an alternate means of entrance and egress. After changing in the dressing rooms on the ground floor near the elevators, they could give wet suits to an attendant who brought them to their rooms or left them in their dressing rooms when dry.

A hotel brochure proclaimed, "the E & S is a popular rendezvous for the younger set during the summer months."

The Warren Hotel's main entry, located on Mercer Avenue, continues to embody the essence of a grand hotel, with its colossal entry columns. In this 1920s view, jardinieres flank the entry. (Photograph courtesy of the Warren Hotel.)

This postcard view shows how the hotel evolved from the Queen Ann Lucas Cottages along Warren Avenue to encompass the property to the south. (Joseph A. Dunn postcard collection.)

A 1920s Warren Hotel brochure illustrates the inviting view from the Mercer Avenue porch over the lawns of the Cavanaugh house, formerly at the corner of Ocean and Mercer Avenues, and to the ocean beyond.

Terra-cotta griffins populate the roof ridges and turrets of the Warren's "Beach House," formerly a private home built for Philadelphia poet Algernon Sydney Logan in the 1890s. (Steve Lacko, photographer.)

Young guests of the Warren Hotel are pictured enjoying a hayride in this 1953 photograph. (Courtesy of the Warren Hotel.)

On the site of the Monmouth House, the Spring Lake Hotel & Realty Co. engaged the Philadelphia firm Watson & Huckel to design the Monmouth Hotel. The new hotel surpassed its predecessor in size and height. The focal point was a central dome, flanked by two polygonal towers. The following photographs are from the collection of Mrs. Jeanne Duggan.

When the Monmouth Hotel opened on August 20, 1903, Rev. Alphonso A.Willits, who had presided at the opening of the Monmouth House, was one of the illustrious 100 guests and a speaker at the formal dinner marking the occasion. The "New Monmouth" was host to thousands of appreciative guests until its closure in 1974. This view of the Monmouth Hotel shows the carriage entrance on Ocean Avenue.

A casual atmosphere was provided in the sun-filled, rattan-furnished lounge.

Parents and onlookers observed a children's dance on the lawn of the Monmouth.

Elegant and comfortable seating groups were featured in the main lobby rotunda, which was flanked by garlanded columns.

The Catholic clergy formed an early morning procession from St. Catharine's Church to the Monmouth Hotel in the 1950s. It became a tradition for priests to hold retreats at the Monmouth in the still-pleasant days between Labor Day and the hotel's official season closure.

The first home to be built on the site of the Monmouth Hotel incorporates the original hotel's cornerstone in its fireplace. It was called "little house on the prairie" when first built by Thomas R. Schwier in 1975. (Courtesy of Dr. Charles Wrege.)

Three

Sites of Worship

In the years before churches were constructed in Spring Lake, history tells us that the faithful worshiped in parlors of hotels and at the Spring Lake Beach Post Office, then located along West Lake Drive to the north of the Hewitt-Wellington Hotel, where a community Protestant Sunday school was conducted. St. Andrew's Sunday school students were grouped on the steps of their church in this 1928 photograph. (Spring Lake Historical Society.)

The cornerstone of the Episcopal Church of the Holy Trinity was laid in the fall of 1880 on ground purchased in 1878, making it Spring Lake's oldest church. Its construction combines Stick style and Gothic features, and its designer remains unknown. Organized as an independent summer chapel by some of Spring Lake's early resort-era investors, it was dedicated on the first Sunday in July 1881. A Philadelphia-made historic Bates and Culley tracker organ with polychromed pipes dating from 1904 graces the sanctuary. (Trustees of Trinity Church.)

A number of architectural gifts in memory of congregants have embellished the church over the years. Here are two impressive, arched stained-glass windows depicting angels and Christ in the garden of Gethsemane. Its history and architectural integrity have earned it a listing on the National Register of Historic Places. (Trustees of Trinity Church.)

Positioned on a serene spot between Spring Lake and the western-facing elevation of the Hastings Square complex, the Spring Lake Presbyterian Church, the 1882 design of Benjamin Linfoot, was a perfect counterpoint to his designs to the east. A pinnacled tower, sheathed in decorative shingles, rose from a stone-based foundation. The building was demolished after being severely damaged by a 1974 fire. This 1903 photograph by G.W. Pach was featured in the presentation album "Spring Lake and the New Monmouth Hotel." (Collection of Mrs. Jeanne Duggan.)

The cornerstone was laid for Spring Lake's first Roman Catholic church, "St. Ann's," in 1884 at the corner of Monmouth and Fifth Avenue. At that time, the "north branch" of Wreck Pond extended to the western side of Monmouth Avenue. Rev. M.L. Glennon, pastor of the Roman Catholic Church of the Holy Spirit in Asbury Park, contracted with William Byrne of Jersey City to build the church according to plans drawn by P.C. Keely, architect. It was later relocated to Fourth Avenue.

St. John's Methodist Church was built by carpenter/builder Herman Reichwein in the summer of 1886 for the Methodist Episcopal Church Association of Colored People upon ground on Fourth Avenue on the banks of the north branch of Wreck Pond donated by John C. Lucas, Pennsylvania Governor Beaver, and William A. Rolin. This *c.* 1895 view shows the church on its site near the bridge between Spring Lake Beach and Villa Park (to the right of the barn; to the left of the picture).

After a fire completely destroyed St. John's Church in 1908, the congregation purchased and moved the original Catholic church, St. Ann's, to its land on Fourth Avenue. When another fire severely damaged the church in 1914, services were held in a tent while Benjamin Wolfson of Long Branch completed repairs to the roof, walls, and bell tower. This photograph from the 80th anniversary of St. John's documents the 1939 reception for Rev. Henry H. Nichols. The church closed after merging with St. Andrew's United Methodist Church.

The cornerstone for St. Andrew's Methodist Church was laid on August 25, 1887, and the structure completed by Herman Reichwein on August 28, 1888. At that time, trustees William Lucas, O.H. Brown, Dr. W. Trout, R.N. Carson, E.V. Patterson, and John Middleton stood before the chancel railing and presented the church, free of debt. The church combines Gothic Revival influences in an asymmetrical Queen Ann form. (Photograph, St. Andrew's United Methodist Church.)

A crenelated bell tower replaced a porte-cochere in 1912, one of few changes made to the church. An amber glow from its many stained-glass windows illuminates the wood-paneled interior. Members of the combined choir fill the sanctuary for a 1940 Christmas concert. Excellent acoustics continue to inspire the church's musical tradition. (Photograph, St. Andrew's United Methodist Church.)

The cornerstone of St. Catharine's Church, designed by Horace Trumbauer, was laid on March 17, 1901. It was built by utilities magnate and philanthropist Martin Maloney in memory of his daughter Catharine, who died at age 17, and his mother, also named Catharine. The temple-fronted Classical revival design features an octagonal dome sheathed in copper. In this September 1955 photograph, a mass and ceremony attended by the Knights of Columbus was held on the plaza and street in front of the church. Not visible, but just south of the plaza is Our Lady of Fatima Shrine, a cruciform path with marble statuary on a triangular plot, dedicated on August 15, 1952.

The interior of St. Catharine's is a treasury of ecclesiastic artwork, with the first murals painted in this country by Prof. Gonippo Raggi (1875–1959), brought here from Rome by Mr. Maloney. The central dome features a depiction of the Pentecost using life-sized figures, with the four evangelists in the panels below. (Courtesy of St. Catharine's-St. Margaret's Parish.)

St. Margaret's Church was built in 1930 as a mission church for St. Catharine's parish after a 1928 cross-burning on the rectory lawn steeled the determination of Msrg. Reilly to expand parish facilities. Designed in the Renaissance Revival Style, it echoes classical motifs found at St. Catharine's. It is the design of Shrewsbury architect Vincent J. Eck. Note the original heavy entry doors of vertical planking in this 1940s photograph.

The interior of St. Margaret's has a folkloric feel, with its stencilled ceiling panels and enormous chamfered and polychromed oak beams. It has an impressive rose window over the main entry with columned spandrels. The basement of the church housed the parish school until 1951. It is the first church in the state to be named after St. Margaret.

This fittingly Classical Revival parish house was built for St. Catharine's parish on Essex Avenue, opposite the church, in 1911 by architect Frank Seeburger. (Photograph, Irving Underhill.)

Msgr. Thomas U. Reilly wears the miter, ring, and cross after the distinct honor of Prothonotary Apostolic was conferred upon him in 1948. Standing on the front steps of St. Catharine's are, from left to right, two men who remain unidentified, Bishop Griffin, Archbishop Walsh (who ordained him in 1918), Msgr. Donhauer, Msgr. Reilly, Msgr. Stanton, and two unidentified parish priests in deacon and subdeacon attire. The unidentified man standing on the steps below wears the insignia of a Papal Marquis.

The groundbreaking for St. Catharine's School took place in September 1951. Sister Agnes Bernadette of the Sisters of St. Joseph of Chestnut Hill, who was in charge of the parish school since 1932, breaks ground with the ceremonial spade as Msgr. Reilly looks on. Also present are Mayor Frank Marucci, Councilman Edward J. Heine, and Fr. Emmanuel Duffy, O.F.M. Present but not pictured was builder Stephen Day. (Bill McGinley, photographer.)

On May 1, 1953, Margaret Baker, a member of Sister Rose Regina's St. Catharine's kindergarten class, reaches out high to place a crown upon Our Lady during a Benediction of the Blessed Sacrament at St. Catharine's School auditorium. (Bill McGinley, photographer; all parish photographs, courtesy of St. Catharine's-St. Margaret's Parish.)

Four

Buildings and Builders

In addition to the natural features that give Spring Lake its distinctive character, the stylistic variation and historic aspects evident in its buildings continue to fascinate and intrigue. The majority of house building activity was conducted by Philadelphians who took an early interest in the area. Examples illustrative of the buildings and builders of Spring Lake will be explored in this section. Members of the Wells, Sickles, and Marburg families are pictured while on a wagon ride outing. Timothy Hurley, the livery stable owner, is the driver in this view given to the Borough of Spring Lake by Elizabeth Justice Chasey. The 1883 Queen Ann styled cottage of Lemuel Wells on Sussex Avenue is in the background.

The cottages built for William C. Hamilton in 1876 were featured in this two-page spread appearing in the 1878 Woolman & Rose Atlas of Monmouth County.

Here, two of the Hamilton Cottages appear with one joined to an 1880s-style Queen Ann structure (in the foreground) by a porch. Note the X-shaped exterior details and the deeply overhanging gable eaves. It appears that these homes were relocated to Atlantic and Third Avenues *c.* 1917.

The atlas plate corresponding to the one on the preceding page shows other views of the Hamilton Cottages.

This 1890s view of an early inn at the corner of First and Sussex Avenues shows the mansard-roofed Ashling Cottage to the west (far left), another of the earliest resort-era homes, the Ocean House, and the Mercer Avenue home of engineer Frederick Anspach, with its distinctively high tower and port-cochere. (Courtesy of Dr. Charles Wrege.)

The octagonal Portuguese Government Pavilion, the design of Herman Schwartzmann of Philadelphia, is depicted as it appeared at the Centennial Exposition. It was used as a resting place for Portuguese visitors to the exposition. (The Print and Photographs Collection, the Free Public Library of Philadelphia.)

Transported to Atlantic Avenue by Dr. J.F. Chaplain of Philadelphia in 1877, the Portuguese Pavilion eventually became a guesthouse. Prior to the construction of the Catholic church, masses were held there. Expansions obscured the airy, gazebo-like features of the building, which was demolished in 1983. (Courtesy of Dr. Charles D. Wrege.)

In 1880, William Golder engaged J.C. Randolph to build two matching inns on his property on Central Avenue. Of the two homes, the easternmost one, now the lovingly-restored White Lilac Inn, is the best preserved, retaining its three-sided porch on both first and second stories. (Courtesy of Mari and Chuck Slocum.)

In the 1880s, developers Golder and Pignueron were actively building boardinghouses in the Villa Park section. This 1950s view shows two examples of that era on Ocean Road.

Early property owners in the Villa Park section moved two state buildings from the Philadelphia Centennial to that locale after the exposition closed and some of the buildings were auctioned off. In this photograph from the Print and Picture Collection, the Free Public Library of Philadelphia, the New Hampshire House is seen as the gabled, three-story building, (second from the left) while the exposition was open.

In November 1876, John Goddard purchased the New Hampshire House to relocate it on Shore Road in Villa Park, where it fronted on Wreck Pond until it was destroyed by fire on April 12, 1962. This late-nineteenth-century photograph documents the elegant vestibule during the occupancy of C.E. Henry Stengel. (Spring Lake Historical Society.)

The Missouri State Pavilion stood on the slope of St. George's Hill in Philadelphia. Its entire first floor was a single room where specimens of minerals and woods were displayed in cases. A ladies' lounge on its second floor was reached through a stair in the prominent tower. The building is the sole remaining Centennial building in Spring Lake on Ocean Road. It was relocated to the Villa Park section in 1877 by Charles Dillingham, whose brother-in-law, Rev. Chandler, also built a summer home on the same block. (The Print and Photographs Collection, the Free Public Library of Philadelphia.)

The porthole windows of this Queen Ann cottage, now on Atlantic Avenue, once looked out upon Wreck Pond. Located on the corner of Central Avenue and Shore Road, it was owned by Brooklyn resident Mrs. Mary Jessup, who sold it to Dr. W.W. Trout. In January 1887, Dr. Trout purchased the home and had it moved to his Atlantic Avenue lot.

Dr. William W. Trout (1854–1932) was a native of Cumberland County, Pennsylvania, who came to Spring Lake as a pharmacist, working in the summers of 1879 and 1880 for the McKelvey drugstore, which he bought out in 1881 and became a partner with Charles Bye. He would move his drugs from the Carleton House to the post office in the winter. He returned to Philadelphia for a medical degree and came back to Spring Lake to practice medicine in 1886. He was a founding trustee of St. Andrew's Church, a councilman, and borough collector, as well as a board of education member. (Richard Napolitan, photographer.)

Mrs. Jessup had the builder/architect Albert V. Porter of Montague Street, Brooklyn, design this expansive cottage on her Central Avenue property in 1888. It featured custom-made cabinetry, woodwork in quarter-oak paneled wainscotting, and corbelled brick chimneys. No longer standing, the home was known as the Stevens guesthouse when captured in this 1956 tax photograph.

In 1885, Philadelphia lawyer Henry C. Townsend had Thomas Gregg build two contiguous three-story homes designed by Philadelphia architect Willis G. Hale at the southeast corner of Monmouth and Second Avenues. The structures were neighbors until the corner home was relocated to Tuttle Avenue, and the eastern home moved one lot west. This postcard view shows the block before the houses were moved. The Gray Swan Inn, which became the Shoreham Hotel, is to the left. (Collection of Joseph A. Dunn.)

This is one of the Townsend cottages of Monmouth Avenue, relocated to Tuttle Avenue in the early part of the twentieth century, as it appeared in the 1950s. Operated as the Sea Crest Inn, its generous proportions and Victorian features continue to be appreciated. (Courtesy of John Kirby.)

The Normandy Inn, also on Tuttle Avenue, was relocated *c.* 1909 from Passaic Avenue when it was purchased by O.H. Brown from the Audenried estate, and later enlarged. The authentically restored inn features a harmonious mix of Queen Ann and Italianate features.

The Normandy Inn's elegant reception room and parlor feature impressive decorative plaster cornices and rosettes. It is on the National Register of Historic Places. (Courtesy of Michael Ingeno.)

In 1882, Thomas B. Shriver, a partner in the Philadelphia Abitoir, had Philadelphia civil engineers and architects Wilson Bros. & Co. prepare plans for this substantial cottage. It was originally built on the northeast corner of Mercer and First Avenues and later moved to the southwest corner of Warren and First Avenues. The exterior shingles were to be stained with burnt Sienna before being dipped in oil. Small panes of stained glass are in the upper sash of the windows to contrast with the clear glass of the lower sashes. Terra-cotta set off each dormer and roof crest. In 1889, a historic meeting of property owners was held in this building which led to the incorporation of Spring Lake as a borough in 1892. (Collection of Elizabeth Robinson, loan to Spring Lake Historical Society.)

Emily B. Chamberlain of Denville, Pennsylvania, contracted with Thomas Gregg to build this impressive dwelling designed by John K. Yarnall on East Lake Avenue in 1882. Note the shingled windmill to the northeast of the house. The cottage of Lemuel Wells is to the east, along Sussex Avenue. (Courtesy of Borough of Spring Lake, gift of the Marucci family.)

The asymmetry and contrasting colors and textures of the Queen Ann style are evident in the carriage house and stable of the Wells Cottage. A fan-shaped sunburst segment adorns the apex of the gable. (Courtesy of Dr. Charles D. Wrege.)

Philadelphia architect Louis C. Hickman designed this impressive Colonial Revival summer cottage on Mercer Avenue for Philadelphia attorney Rufus E. Shapley for occupancy in April 1893. H.P. Brown was the builder. (Pach Collection; Spring Lake Historical Society.)

This view of the Hamilton House Inn, c. 1905, illustrates how the enlargement and addition of decorative shingles over the original siding Victorianized the structure. Note the jewel-like sunburst designs in the upper sash. (Pach Collection; Spring Lake Historical Society.)

This charming Queen Ann cottage called "Red Top," is located on Remsen Avenue in the Como section, with South Boulevard and Lake Como to the north. Early area developers cleared a large sand hill in the 1880s to create ocean vistas from the backlands and terraced lots. It illustrates how the blocks were laid out in diagonally shaped lots to maximize views to the ocean. (Courtesy of Dr. Charles D. Wrege.)

The Como Railroad Station was built by Como area developers Yard and Force in 1887 at the intersection of Pitney and Fourth Avenues. Area residents protested the railroad's refusal to make stops at the station in the 1920s, although it was a stop on the Coast Cities trolley run. The station was demolished in 1934. (Collection of Joseph A. Dunn.)

In 1886, William M. Force had Lewis W. Randolph of Plainfield build this two-and-one-half-story frame and stone house at the corner of Pitney and Howell Avenues, seen here in a 1956 tax photograph. According to the designs of R.H. Rowden of Newark, the home's circular tower was built of a dark, fine brownstone with a rough face finish. At its base, the tower's walls were to be 16 inches thick.

The L-shaped Hewitt-Wellington complex began as pairs of adjoining, three-story cottages on the northwest corner of Second Avenue, and two adjoining ones along Monmouth Avenue. They were built for Henry C. Townsend and his wife, Georgiana L., in 1889 by builder Herman Reichwein and were let individually. The Seaholm (facing south) and the Hewitt Wellington eventually merged under one name.

WILSON EYRE, JR.
Architect of many Phila. and New York residences, college buildings, churches, etc.

HORACE TRUMBAUER
Architect Widener Cripples' Instn. and homes of Widener, Elkins, Berwind, Harrison, Huhn, et al.

EDWARD HAZLEHURST
Arch't Odd Fellows' Temple; Residences Wm. Wood, Dan'l Baugh, J. F. Sinnott, R. H. Foerderer

ADDISON HUTTON
Architect. Lecturer on Architecture, Univ. of Pa. Fellow American Institute of Architects

LOUIS CARON HICKMAN
Archt. Keneseth Israel Temple, Potts Bldg., etc. Remodeled and rebuilt Phila. Stock Exch., 1902

FRANK EATON NEWMAN
Newman, Woodman & Harris, Arch. Rittenhouse Club; Corn Ex. Nat. Bank; 1st City Troop Armory

EDGAR VIGNERS SEELER

WILLIAM LIGHTFOOT PRICE

WILLIS GAYLORD HALE

This composite page of portraits of engineers and architects from *King's Philadelphia and Notable Philadelphians* (1902) depicts many talented contemporaries active in designing buildings in Spring Lake. (Author's collection.)

CHARLES HENRY CRAMP
Pres. Wm. Cramp & Sons Ship & Eng. Bldg. Co.
Builders of War and Merchant Vessels

JOHN LUCAS
John Lucas & Co. Dir. Camden & Atlantic R. R.
Fdr. Gibsboro' White Lead, Zinc and Color Works

MARTIN MALONEY
Capitalist
Director in several Corporations

EDWIN SAMUEL CRAMP
V.-P. & Dir. Wm. Cramp & Sons Ship & Engine
Bldg. Co. Harbor Com'r. Dir. Maritime Exchange

RUFUS EDMONDS SHAPLEY
Shapley & Ballard, Traction and Corp. Lawyers
Author. Co-Editor "Library of Wit and Humor"

JAMES GAY GORDON
Lawyer. Ex-Judge Philadelphia County
Ex-Justice Court of Common Pleas No. 3

RICHARD McCALL CADWALADER
Lawyer. Author. V.-P. Genealogical Soc. Pres.

WILLIAM LUCAS
John Lucas & Co., Manufacturers

CHARLES MOSELEY SWAIN
President City Trust, Safe Deposit & Surety Co

The extensive listing of merchants and investors in the 1902 *King's Notable Philadelphians* revealed an impressive roster of individuals who had considerable interests in Spring Lake.

This elegant cottage on the corner of Morris and First Avenues was designed in 1892 by Willis G. Hale for Martin Maloney. Originally built on the western half of the block to the north, it was moved across the street when Mr. Maloney acquired the remainder of the block to build his mansion, "Ballingarry." (Spring Lake Historical Society.)

The magnificent Swain house on Passaic and First Avenues has remained relatively unchanged since it was first built. Note the sunburst over the main entry. Its builder remains unknown, but its dormered turrets are reminiscent of Bruce Price's designs for the Carleton Hotel. (Pach Collection; Spring Lake Historical Society.)

This unusual view from the Spring Lake Historical Society's Maloney Collection shows the Ballingarry mansion under construction in the winter of 1899.

Snow gives Ballingarry's Morris Avenue elevation a dream-like glow in this view by Nettie MeGill.

The mansion was built on a terraced site and set back within the confines of a 10-foot-tall wrought-iron fence The following photographs are from a 1903 presentation album by G.W. Pach entitled "Ballingarry and Spring Lake." (Author's collection.)

This view of a section of the drawing room gives a hint of the sumptuous interior treatment.

The library featured fine artwork, such as the reproduction of the *Madonna of the Chair* from St. Charles Borromeo above the bookcase, as well as other paintings.

The breakfast room, pictured with its table fully set, was elegant in every detail.

This view of Seawood from the "park" shows the impressive mansion, built as the country estate of Samuel and Adelaide Heilner in 1904. The house and outbuildings for the 15-acre estate were designed by Newman and Harris. The following series of photographs is from the Spring Lake Historical Society.

Skillfully executed newel-posts in the shape of woodland animals were carved out of red oak for Seawood's dramatic main stairway.

The mantle in the "play room" featured ornamental plasterwork in a classically inspired design. The wooden benches flanking the hearth gave a sense of intimacy to the room.

A thatched gatehouse at Pitney and Second Avenues led into the property, which also had a "tearoom" (i.e. a raised gazebo) and well house with a "sweep" and oaken bucket, each roofed in thatch. (Collection of Joseph A. Dunn.)

The house built by H.H. Moore for Mary Polak of New York still stands on Brighton Avenue. This *c.* 1905 view was taken by Nettie Megill.

In 1904, Henry W. Rogers had Philadelphia architect Wilson Eyre design this impressive home on an oceanfront block bounded by Monroe Avenue to the south. It was later the home of the Roebling family. All master rooms overlooked lawns and the ocean. The house was reduced in size when the block was subdivided in the 1950s.

This rustic bungalow of Thomas B. Wells, on Vroom and First Avenues, displayed many Craftsman style features. During the summer of 1918, famed tenor Enrico Caruso was a guest of New Yorker Park Benjamin, who was occupying this cottage while Caruso was concertizing at nearby Ocean Grove.

This interior view of the Wells bungalow epitomizes the unpretentious grandeur and informality of the Craftsman style. Here, a study adjoins a living hall. Both are enveloped by a soaring, beamed ceiling.

This rustic frame bungalow on Ludlow Avenue was built for Grace L. Neafie. Set back atop a wooded lot, it was designed by Addison and Newman in 1915.

This rustic cabin on a wooded Fourth Avenue site belonged to the Woolley family, prior to the construction of Valendora Court in the 1920s. (Collection of Richard Napolitan.)

This enchanting rustic lodge now known as the Hollycroft Inn on North Boulevard, South Belmar, was built in 1908 by Newark resident William D. Ripley when that location was the northernmost street in Spring Lake's Como section. It was designed by Newark architects Eugene A. McMurray and W. Pell Pulis. Originally named "the Enclosure," the house is set atop a hill overlooking Lake Como. The hill was once covered by pine trees, which gave way to oak trees in the 1930s. Sometime between 1930 and the 1940s, the house was faced with iron stone from Allaire. The rustic theme is carried through the interior by unhewn wood beams on the walls and ceiling on the main floor and by a two-story brick-faced chimney, which rises through the upper stairwell and incorporates a blue and white punchbowl from the St. Louis Exposition. (Collection of Gurney Lord.)

The unpretentious simplicity of the early year-round homes of Spring Lake is evident in the Jersey Avenue home of the Megill family. With her mother waiting on a porch rocker, Nettie simply inscribed "home" under this photograph in her album.

In this 1956 tax photograph, the Mission styled Valendora Court is a 1920s residential enclave featuring these diminutive homes in a woodland setting.

Five

Spring Lake Landscapes

Perhaps the most enduring image of the community is that of the freshwater, spring-fed lake that inspired the town's name. The Spring Lake Beach Improvement Company directors dedicated the lands around the lake as a public park and set about planting trees and creating paths in 1875. This Pach photograph, *c.* 1903, was often featured in albums and postcards.

The paths around the eastern border of the lake were the first to be furnished with a plank-walk, which was then extended to the western side. By 1878, a rustic bridge was built connecting Fourth Avenue at West Lake to Passaic Avenue. This view is from a 1895 railroad guide to Spring Lake. (Collection of Elizabeth P. Robinson.)

The bridge at Fourth Avenue was later rebuilt *c.* 1914 with a higher center span and featured an elaborate "birdcage" design. The pattern created by the supporting beams, outriggers, and fanciful railings displays the artistry of this naturalistic style of bridge-building. Efforts led by the Spring Lake Improvement Association led to the formation of a Shade Tree Commission, and the Olmstead Bros. firm was consulted, although it is unclear if the firm drew up a planting plan.

The portion of Spring Lake's Divine Park, named after the borough's first superintendent, R.T. Divine, was by the 1880s a peninsula park, dotted with small icehouses for the convenience of the property owners. This rustic gazebo, pictured here in an early-twentieth-century view, sat near the location of the present tennis courts. (Nettie Megill, photographer.)

This photograph captures the serenity of a late afternoon view of wild geese on Spring Lake, c. 1912. (Nettie Megill, photographer.)

Around 1902, a second cedarwood footbridge was built over Spring Lake, connecting Mercer Avenue to East Lake. The center, with its commanding view of the lake and surroundings, became a favored spot for informal photographic portraits. In this view, the gentle breeze is almost palpable as Nettie Megill captured her friend, a Miss Hoag, in her strolling finery.

The mute swans that grace the lakes and ponds of Spring Lake were a gift to the borough *c.* 1913. These lovely creatures have endured, despite the sometimes careless treatment they are given by humans, their fishing apparatus, and dogs. This picture by Mike Jones shows the sheltered spot chosen by a pair of swans for their nest.

This publicity photograph, which appeared in a *c.* 1930s chamber of commerce and hotel literature, shows two young girls feeding bread to the swans, a practice now known to be detrimental. The perimeter of the lake was lined with "granite-crystal" stones in a Spring Lake Improvement Association beautification project in the 1920s. (Mrs. Jeanne Duggan, photographer.)

A picturesque feature of the lake was the presence of several peaked-roofed wooden boathouses, adjoining plankwalk docks. Phoebe Edwards Dunn was photographed on the steps of the boathouse of the Seaholm Inn in this *c.* 1914 photograph. (Edwards family album, courtesy of Jennie Lee Aitkenhead.)

Standing on the front lawn of the Seaholm along West Lake Avenue, Phoebe Edwards Dunn glances cautiously toward the pair of black swans to her left. The first pair was donated in 1912 by Mrs. Jasper Lynch, but did not acclimate. (Courtesy of Jennie Lee Aitkenhead.)

Waterlillies continue to proliferate in the relative shallow water of the peninsula near Passaic Avenue and East Lake as they did in 1912. (Nettie Megill, photographer.)

Robert Winemiller (left), Russel Hurden (center), and Howard Parker seem delighted with their catch of 75 fish in this 1947 photograph. (Courtesy of Chief Russel "Bunky" Hurden.)

This sheet of Spring Lake view stamps, *c.* 1910, sold in stapled books of 50 stamps for 5¢ and was distributed by H.P. Lombard, Toms River, New Jersey. It featured popular images of the town, many of which also appeared as postcards. Before postal officials ultimately prohibited the use of such "pasters," the view stamps added flourish to correspondence. (Spring Lake Historical Society.)

This Queen Ann-style boat/carriage house was built for a Mr. Gallagher on Ocean Road, fronting on the north branch of Wreck Pond in the 1880s. (Eileen McLaughlin, photographer.)

Wreck Pond, a brackish inlet, forms a natural division between Spring Lake and Sea Girt to the south. The desire to exert control over the entire perimeter of the lake caused the Sea Girt and Spring Lake Improvement Co., successor to the Spring Lake Beach Improvement Co., with land holdings in southern Spring Lake and present-day Sea Girt, to envision the two tracts joined as one community *c.* 1890. The eventual subdivision of Spring Lake Beach from Wall Township in 1892 precluded that from occurring, leaving control of the borders in two jurisdictions. Timothy Hurley, owner of much of the land adjoining the pond, began dredging the pond in 1913 to fill in the lowlands and graded roads. There was an unsuccessful petition circulated to rename the pond "Lake Garda," which is the largest lake in the northern Italian lake region which includes the Como section's namesake, Lake Como, and to rename Ocean Road "Neptune Boulevard." By 1931, the two towns took steps to install apparatus to regulate the water level of the pond so that unsightly mud flats would be covered at all times. This photograph by Mike Jones captures the expanse of the pond, looking at its widest point toward Sea Girt.

This 1956 tax photograph of the estate called "Swanhurst," formerly the Worral cottage, shows the ivy-covered sycamore trees forming their canopy over Mercer Avenue. The property has a picturesque carriage house, designed in 1899 by Edgar V. Seeler and once featured parterres and a greenhouse extending to Warren Avenue.

This L-shaped classical arbor spanned the western edge of the Essex and Sussex site, extending behind the Queen Ann houses along Essex Avenue. It framed views of the lake and surrounded a central pool ringed with hollyhocks. The semi-private garden could be seen from First Avenue. (Spring Lake Historical Society.)

From left to right, Helen and Jack VanCleaf and Grace and Sadie Voorhees pause to smell a rose on the Megill family porch. A plankwalk set over the grass sufficed instead of paving.

The Edwards family home on St. Clair Avenue and Fourth Avenue has, since 1910, been called "Cartref," Welsh for "our house." It was formerly called "the Farm" by Judge James Gay Gordon of Philadelphia, who had it enlarged to create a library. In this 1962 photograph, newlyweds Jennie Lee Edwards and Rennie Aitkenhead are framed in an ivy arbor. Both the arbor and tradition continue to be propagated. (Courtesy of Jennnie Lee Aitkenhead.)

Two members of the Nesbitt family engage in conversation while resting on a boardwalk bench just north of the forerunner to the present South Pavilion at Atlantic Avenue. The expanse of non-commercial boardwalk and dune plantings is a key feature of the Spring Lake landscape. (Spring Lake Historical Society.)

The Queen Ann-style house that has for decades been known as "Green Gables" is the last remaining home enjoying an uninterrupted block of Ocean Avenue frontage, seen here in this 1956 tax photograph. The estate, built by Isabella Wallace around the turn of the century, has long been known for its fine gardens. Its well-tended border of perimeter plantings includes a hedge-enclosed vegetable and cutting garden.

The site of Martin Maloney's legendary estate, Ballingarry, is marked by a distinctive 10-foot-high fence that surrounds the perimeter of the entire block. Although the mansion was demolished in 1955, a deed restriction placed by Mr. Maloney required that the fence and landscape features be retained to enhance the property and surrounding neighborhood. A central path, laid out along an east-west axis, features gardens and many architectural features that remain in this strictly private enclave. The following pictures are from a presentation album by G.W. Pach in 1903. (Author's collection.)

The classicism evident in the architecture of Ballingarry was carried through to the splendid gardens of the property. A piazza facing west offered a view down the center of the block-square property.

Stairs frame views of the garden beds. Mr. Maloney, who employed a full-time gardener, Mr. Plangere, was keenly interested in horticulture and active in an early Spring Lake garden club. Waterlilies in a circular pool added exotic interest to the gardens. Note the rusticwork bench to the left in the foreground.

The gardens of the Lowlands estate, designed in 1904 by Wilson Eyre for Henry Welsh Rogers, included a rose garden and grape arbor–lined path from Monroe Avenue. A somewhat sheltered environment was created for the rose gardens by situating them to the west of the broad north-south axis of the home, which was built on a bluff overlooking the ocean.

This postcard view shows how the Lake House site was transformed into a public park after the hotel was demolished in 1904. In 1913, the park was named "Potter Park" to commemorate local businessman and Mayor William H. Potter, who died in 1907 while in office. The park now features a substantial gazebo at its center. (Collection of Joseph A. Dunn.)

The park-like Heilner estate "Seawood" displays a more naturalistic approach that was taking hold in American landscape design. Research confirms that the gardens captured in these 1916 photographs in the collection of the Spring Lake Historical Society were designed by Clarence Fowler (1870–1935). He left his studies at Harvard University to join the New York practice of Ferrucio Vitale in 1911 and then formed his own firm in 1916, from which he achieved many important country estate commissions in the New York-New Jersey area.

This view from the ocean porch of Seawood captures the commanding view over the gardens and grounds, facing toward the ocean. Note how the "loggia," or open, covered porch, suggests a casual elegance, with its climbing and cascading ivy.

An artful photographic effect was created using the image reflected in the gazing ball set in the Seawood gardens, in which the arch of a trellis is captured. The estate was demolished and subdivided in 1959.

Herringbone-brick–patterned walks led to the parterre gardens bright with daylilies. This formality was offset by the expanse of lawn, edged by sheltering woods. The lovely gardens and home were utilized by the community-minded Heilners for "lawn fetes," including Women's Club, public library and Ann May Hospital Alliance events.

This photograph captures Fowler's unusual and inventive "dial" garden, composed of planted materials that form Roman numerals. A diagonal, outward-projecting rod cast an ever-changing shadow on the numerals below.

Informal, rustic stone steps lead to a contemplative garden setting.

A stone-edged fish pond, set near the easternmost terminus of the property, provides a secluded and tranquil spot.

In the background to the right of this photograph of Nettie Megill and her friend Grace Voorhees is the brick stack of the North Spring Lake Water Co., which fronted Washington Avenue and which is the site of the current Police and Fire Building. Her hand-inked caption reads "coming through the rye," referring to the native grasses let to grow on the undeveloped lots.

"Saewic," the Howell Avenue home of Mr. and Mrs. Alexander Julian Hemphill, sat high on a terraced site, with gardens protected from the ocean winds by the home itself as well as perimeter boxwood hedges. The gardens featured a central fountain and flower beds in quadrants filled with roses around which perimeter plantings were placed. These gardens were designed *c*. 1916 by the Olmstead Brothers' firm. Research confirms that planting plans exist for this significant property, which was destroyed in a 1956 fire during a nor'easter storm. A delicate trellis that incorporates birdhouses survives, now along Lorraine Avenue. This is a view of Saewic featured in a 1930s promotional pamphlet on Spring Lake.

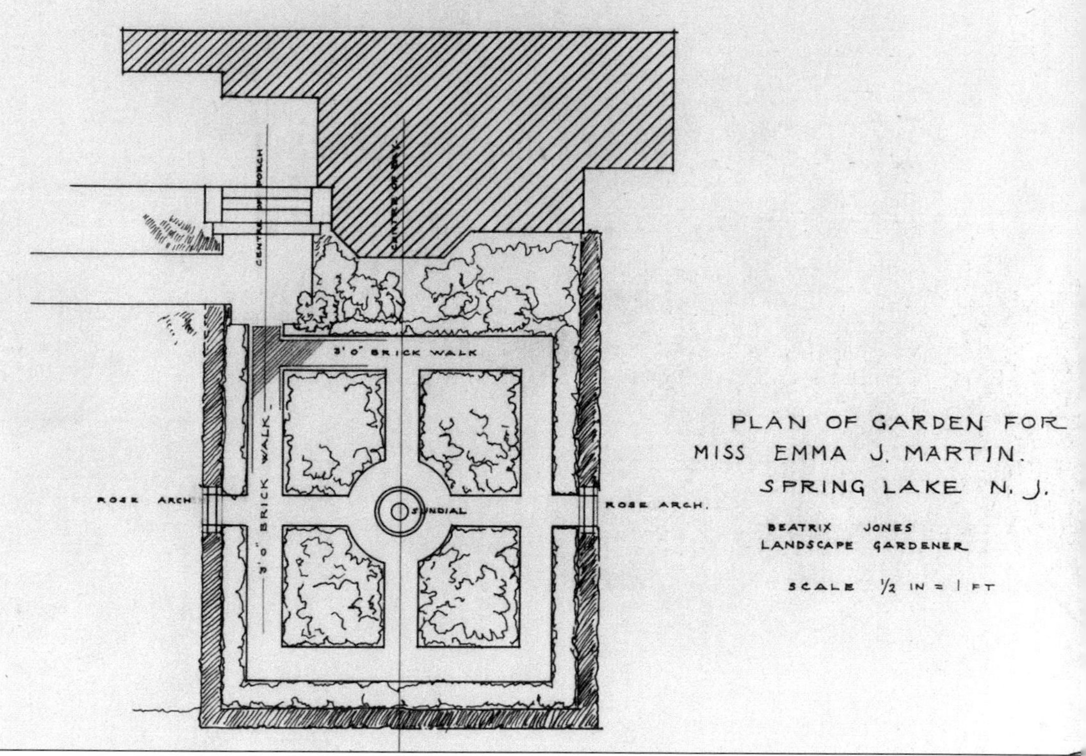

Similar to the Hemphill's garden layout was the Washington Avenue garden of Miss Emma Martin, who was active in Spring Lake beautification projects and aware of the Oldstead's park designs in Newark and the Oranges through friends in that area. Her Victorian home had a sideyard that faced east. The challenge of creating a garden that would be in a setback sideyard was explored by Beatrix Jones (1872–1959) in this design from the Reef Point Gardens Collection of the University of California at Berkeley. Through French doors that once led out from the dining room, one could enter the classically laid-out garden, with its intersecting brick paths, centrally-placed sundial, and enclosing hedge, to enjoy the planting of white roses. Beatrix Jones created this intimately scaled garden at an early stage of her distinguished career and before her 1913 marriage to Prof. Max Farrand. The vestiges of the garden survived until the 1970s, when unsuspecting owners cleared the remains of the garden, relocating the bricks into a den fireplace and hearth. (Documents Collection, University of California at Berkeley.)

Lake Como, once known as "Three Cornered Pond," is a brackish body of water that was originally entirely within the confines of the Como section of Spring Lake until its northern border became part of South Belmar in 1924. (Courtesy of Dr. Charles D. Wrege.)

A crowd of interested onlookers gathered to watch a promotional event sponsored by the developers of Ocean Gardens, on lands bordering the improved south and west sides of Lake Como. (Spring Lake Historical Society.)

The Spring Lake Improvement Association initiated a dredging operation that extended into 1931 to fill in 20 acres of lowlands around and west of Third Avenue, including an area used as the Como dump. The substantially deepened pond was to become a wildlife refuge. (*Spring Lake Gazette*, June 1931, and photo, Spring Lake Historical Society.)

Six

Community Places

Spring Lake's Classical Revival schoolhouse, now Borough Hall, at Warren and Fifth Avenues, was designed by Brouse and Arend in 1897. The grassy park opposite was used by the children during recess. Dr. Harry W. Mountz, a teacher since 1908, became the school's principal in 1914. When enrollment at the four-room school approached 220 pupils, the question of building an extension to the school was put up for referendum in 1918, but was defeated in an election in which only men could vote. It was felt that the school's location was not convenient to the families of the town. The following year, women candidates made unsuccessful but historic runs for seats on the school board. The school was decorated for "Welcome Home Day" in this 1918 photograph. (Courtesy of the Borough of Spring Lake.)

Upper Left: In this cartoon that appeared in the local newspaper, the *Coast Star*, in 1918, Uncle Sam takes his hat off to a resourceful woman who shakes his hand while holding a hoe in the other.
Upper Right: The Men's League for Women's Suffrage, of which Spring Lake summer resident ex-Governor Franklin Fort was an active member, purchased a little yellow car named "the Voter" in which suffrage worker Eva Ward travelled throughout the state. Her Monmouth County advent was heralded in the *Coast Star* in 1915.

Troops bid farewell from the train station during World War I. (Courtesy of the Borough of Spring Lake.)

The defeat of the referendum spurred Mayor O.H. Brown to offer an assemblage of lots he owned on Tuttle Avenue to the board of education substantially below their market price for a new school. H. Arend was the architect for the ten-room school, which opened to students in January 1923. In 1962, the board of education named the school after Dr. Mountz upon his retirement after 48 years as principal. The school was expanded in 1971 through the efforts of the "NEED" Committee, which supported the expansion of the school. With an addition to the east, designed by Flatt and Poole, ten additional classrooms were provided as well as separate art and music rooms, and a newly-equipped gymnasium. A library/learning center was created in the former gymnasium. (Courtesy of the Board of Education.)

Female students at Spring Lake's Public School were in patriotic attire to participate in county-wide Maypole drills as part of the Welcome Home Day celebrations.

Enlisted men back from World War I gathered in front of the H.H. Moore offices on Third and Passaic Avenues for this group picture on Welcome Home Day, September 18, 1918. They were awarded custom-made war medals. It was also announced on that day that a memorial Community House would be built for Spring Lake, as a tribute to the veterans and all those who aided in the war effort. (Courtesy of Richard Napolitan.)

The community house concept as a "living memorial" was being advocated by the National Committee of Memorial Buildings, which sent a representative, Dr. Eugene Rodman Shippen of New York, to speak to interested residents who gathered in the assembly room of Fire Co. No. 1 on the evening of March 17, 1919. Urged by the newly formed Women's Club, residents embraced the idea. On October 29, 1921, Mayor Brown, who pledged $100,000 towards the building fund, broke ground for the house on land which he donated. Spring Lake Historical Society.

This picturesque view of the Madison Avenue entry to the Community House illustrates the dignity of the building, designed by architect Frank E. Newman and constructed by Horace H. Moore in the English Tudor style. It is a structure that incorporates a library, attractive club meeting and reception rooms, and a theatre. The millstone in the park at the west corner is from the Nesbitt Mill, Farmingdale, New Jersey. (Spring Lake Historical Society.)

Mrs. Adeline Heilner, a founder of the Woman's Club and library, stands at the library desk, at which is seated Miss Martha Johnson, the librarian in this 1940s photograph. On the anniversary of its first year of existence, the Woman's club presented the town with a 2,000-volume library, then housed in the Langthorne Cottage, one of the homes eventually removed from the Community House site in 1920. The new library temporarily relocated to the council chambers at the Washington Avenue borough hall until the Community House was complete in 1923. (Spring Lake Historical Society.)

The play *A Woman of Character* was an early production of the theatre, which also included among its varied range of offerings motion pictures, operatic programs by Beaumont and Vivian Glass, and the Spring Lake Sinfonietta, as well as Paul Robeson, one of several renown performers who appeared at the Community House while in the area to perform at Ocean Grove's auditorium. (Spring Lake Historical Society.)

In 1903, Mrs. Albionia Whartenby of Philadelphia had Brouse and Arend design a hospital/convalescent home in memory of her daughter, Ann May Robinson, at the corner of First and Vroom Avenues and a substantial home for herself on the northeast corner of Worthington and First Avenues. Seen here *c.* 1912, the Ann May Memorial Hospital began under the auspices of the Women's Southern Pennsylvania Homeopathic Hospital, but attained its own New Jersey charter in 1905. It was modernized in 1923, continuing its largely altruistic work in Spring Lake until 1930, when its medical and nursing staff joined the new Fitkin Memorial Hospital in Neptune. A fragment of the cornerstone of Ann May Hospital was placed within the Fitkin Memorial cornerstone. (Nettie Megill, photographer.)

Florence L. and Frederic A. Duggan were photographed on the lawn of their Washington Avenue home with their young son, Frederic L., in the 1890s. The Canadian native owned the Monmouth Hotel, the Imperial Porcelain Works of Trenton, and Manasqan and was also active in social and civic affairs in the borough. (Courtesy of Mrs. Jeanne Duggan.)

To commemorate Frederic A. Duggan after he died in an automobile accident in 1929, expiring in an ambulance he had donated to the fledgling first-aid squad, his wife and son had this attractive First Aid Squad building constructed as a living memorial in 1930. The building, designed by Henry Schmieder, may be the first of its kind in the United States and Canada. The survivors of the Morro Castle Disaster were brought here on September 8, 1934.

Members of Goodwill Fire Co. were pictured in the Ballingarry garden, *c.* 1915; they are, from left to right, as follows: Stanley Curtis, Scotty Morton, Clarence D. Nesbitt, George Cauffman, Edward White, George Stillwell, Mr. Yates, Frank Marucci, Oliver S. Camp, Harry Nesbitt, Chris Estelle, George Evans, with Martin Maloney Osborn holding an axe. The fire company occupied the old borough hall on Washington Avenue. It was replaced by the Police and Fire Headquarters in 1991. (Courtesy of the Borough of Spring Lake.)

Engine Co. No. 1 members gathered outside their former firehouse on Fifth Avenue The Queen Ann building, c. 1892, was replaced with a brick building in 1959 at the same location. (Collection of Richard Napolitan.)

Seven
At the Beach

The beachfront is one of Spring Lake's most precious assets. Its surroundings have been the subject of much change over the years. This chapter explores past and present sites in the beach vicinity, from south to north. The people in the group pictured on an August weekend in 1911 seem to be enjoying themselves, despite attire that seems so confining to us today. (Collection of Elizabeth P. Robinson.)

The past tradition of area farmers coming east to celebrate "Sea Day" on the second Saturday in August was captured in this lantern slide image from the 1890s by John S. Neary, Trenton. The amateur photographer reportedly won national awards for his work. (Courtesy of the Borough of Spring Lake.)

This postcard view shows the fishing pier of the Rod and Gun Club, established in 1887, which gave "Pier Beach" its name. The pier was extended another 200 feet in 1929, but later was removed after storm and fire damage. All postcard views in this chapter are from the collection of Joseph A. Dunn, unless noted otherwise.

The Allaire Hotel was a large frame building constructed in the 1880s, with additions by Herman Reichwein. Bandcourses of shingles in contrasting shapes gave variety to the exterior, and the main entry faced south on Union Avenue.

Willow chairs in the lobby underscored the casual seasonal interior of the Allaire Hotel, which was demolished in 1989.

This early pavilion extended over the beach along the area south of the Monmouth Hotel.

Poles supporting swimming ropes are visible in this postcard beachfront scene.

Mrs. Clara Wohlforth and her fluffy white terrier join her husband, Martin, on the Spring Lake beach in 1917. Mr. Wohlforth, the operator of the Atlantic Theater, an early airdome, and later the Ritz, was a pioneer and early advocate of the motion picture business. (Courtesy of Robert Wohlforth.)

The predecessor of today's south pavilion was a frame structure incorporating bathhouses and shops, seen in this early-1900s view. The Spring Lake Improvement Association constructed a series of shelters such as the one to the right to screen children from the sun.

A bather looks up toward the photographer in the gallery above in this interesting interior view of the south pavilion from the 1920s. (Courtesy of the Borough of Spring Lake.)

This view of the brick and tile South Pavilion designed by E. Henry Schmieder in 1928 shows the enlarged and improved bathing facilities.

A miniature golf range was located at the southwest corner of Atlantic and Ocean Avenues. An ordinance was enacted in 1931 in response to concerns over this and the showing of movies on Sundays at the neighboring Ritz Theatre. The message on this card, postmarked 1937, reads, "Have not found the millionaire but still on the lookout. Having a grand time."

John Colrick, Notre Dame's nine-letterman and star end on Knute Rockne's football teams, is surrounded by family in this 1930s souvenir photograph by the Thorne Studio. His sister Mary Ellen sits next to him; his brother, Edward, holds baby Thomas McDonald; and his eldest sister, Margaret Colrick McDonald, sits to the right. (Author's collection.)

In this c. 1913 view, Clara Wohlforth pauses to enjoy a cooling breeze from the eastern-facing second-story porch over Hill's drugstore, which offered seasonal apartments. The family later purchased the Osborn farmhouse. (Collection of Robert Wohlforth.)

Julia Wohlforth sits in the unenclosed ticket booth of the Atlantic Theatre, an early airdrome. Running the seasonal theater involved all members of the Wohlforth family.

Vestiges of the Neo Classical grandeur that exemplified the hotel district are apparent in the colossal, temple-fronted facade of Hill's Pharmacy and Tea Room, at the corner of Atlantic and First Avenues. The Atlantic Theatre is visible to the south along First Avenue.

The Ritz Theatre, on the south side of Atlantic Avenue between Ocean and First Avenues, was built by Martin Wohlforth in 1920 as a fully enclosed theater after his airdrome was defeated by unpredictable weather and the advent of daylight savings time. Robert Wohlforth, who became a celebrated journalist and writer, recalled his childhood experiences in his parents' theaters in essays entitled, "A Nickelodeon Childhood" in the *New Yorker* magazine in 1938.

Foliate columns with torchieres above flanked the wide brick path leading to the Monmouth Hotel's oceanfront entry in this 1928 postcard view.

Joseph A. Dunn (center) is joined by his sisters (to his right), the Romanoa sisters (to his left), and a summer friend in a 1928 Sunday afternoon view.

This view from the dunes to the block between Sussex and Mercer Avenues shows the northern side of one of the Essex and Sussex cottages in the far left corner. (Courtesy of Dr. Charles D. Wrege.)

This view of the oceanfront block between Sussex and Mercer Avenues was taken before the 1909 fire that destroyed Spring Lake's original Breakers Hotel (second from the right). In the years after this view was taken, the house on the corner, an original Hamilton Cottage, was moved to Washington Avenue.

This view down Mercer Avenue from an 1895 railroad guide to Spring Lake shows the many attractive homes lining the street. A wooden pole in the foreground supports wiring that carried electricity to the homes. (Courtesy of Elizabeth P. Robinson.)

The North and South Pavilions were each equipped with pumps for providing water for street-spraying operations; Ocean Avenue was paved in 1921. It was reported ten years later that the Coast Cities Co. would replace the solid rubber tires on their buses with pneumatic ones to reduce noise. (Underhill & Underhill, photographers; collection of Mrs. Jeanne Duggan.)

This photograph from a cottage rental booklet by P.C. Brown featured the impressive turnout of Col. J.M. Schoonmaker. (Collection of Richard Napolitan.)

In 1900, Colonel Schoonmaker of Pittsburg had Brouse & Arend design this oceanfront cottage on the corner of Passaic Avenue. William H. Norris was the builder. In this 1956 tax photograph, winter preparations were underway to protect the shrubbery from damaging salt spray and wind.

The original Bath & Tennis Club built by the Casino Co. was the 1898 design of Horace Trumbauer. The building, which provided an exclusive setting for social and recreational activities of the town's elite, featured an extensive veranda, ballroom, pool, and lockers. (G.W. Pach, author's collection.)

By 1919, in order to expand its overcrowded facilities, Donald Ach drew up plans to enlarge the pool and create a children's pool, additional bathhouses, tennis courts, and a pergola, made possible by Martin Maloney's agreement to sell the club the remaining lots which he held to safeguard the view from Ballingarry. The stairway on Ocean Avenue was demolished and a tunnel built under Ocean Avenue connecting the club to its private beach. (Collection of Mrs. Jeanne Duggan.)

This 1905 postcard view shows people strolling along the boardwalk with stacks of lumber on the dunes in the distance. Wooden jetties began to be installed off the beachfront in the early 1910s in a shore protection effort.

Two members of the Edwards family were stylishly dressed for a beachfront stroll in this *c.* 1914 photograph. (Courtesy of Jennie Lee Aitkenhead.)

In 1957, Mrs. Susie Linden, then Mrs. James Lowell Oakes, founded the Green Gables Croquet Club on her lovely oceanfront property after being inspired to do so at her daughter Diane's wedding reception on the grounds. With a nucleus of enthusiastic friends, the club held weekly matches on the manicured lawns of her Green Gables estate. Here she and her husband, Mr. James Lowell Oakes, are pictured on the mall.

Mrs. Linden retained an abiding interest in croquet until her death in 1997. Photographer Mike Jones took this rooftop view of the annual tournament in 1996. The croquet malls' special bent grass has been replaced with conventional grass by the property's new owners, who plan to continue and enhance the property's tradition of beautifully landscaped grounds.

After the Breakers fire of 1909, this early hotel formerly known as the Wilburton-by-the-Sea, named after Brighton developer Wilbur Tuttle, became the new Breakers, a name that has continued in use to the present.

The early-twentieth-century English Tudor home at the corner of St. Clair and Ocean Avenues was cloaked in mist in this 1956 tax photograph. The house has been extensively remodeled since this time, but its corbelled chimneys indicate its vintage. Note the arched trellis over the entry.

This postcard view shows the nature of the swimming facilities at the north end before the new pavilion was constructed.

This view of the North Pavilion pool shows the expansive swimming pool and second-floor breezeway provided in E. Henry Schmieder's 1931-inspired design.

Both pavilions feature decorative terra-cotta wall plaques that enliven the buff brick exterior with their naturalistic and nautical themes. This example is from the North Pavilion, which has especially large and handsome polychromed tiles, now in need of preservation.

This 1938 photograph from the Asbury Park Press shows cars parked along Ocean Avenue outside the North Pavilion. (Spring Lake Historical Society.)

This Stick Style life saving station, now a private home on Pitney and Second Avenues, was built between 1878–79 near Worthington Avenue, following the design of Francis W. Chandler, who designed 20 such stations throughout the nation. (Courtesy Mildred Colyard.) In the inset, Captain Samuel Ludlow was the keeper of the U.S. Lifesaving Station from 1862–1881. He donated land for the burial of shipwrecked seamen and a Methodist church along the section of Church Street that extends to Spring Lake Heights. (Collection of Louise S. Ludlow, on loan to the Spring Lake Historical Society by descendant Nancy Seitz.)

In 1896, another life saving station, later used as a Coast Guard station, was built at Worthington and Ocean Avenues. It was modeled on the Quonochontaug, Rhode Island station designed in 1891 by Albert B. Bibb, one of 21 designed by him. The Spring Lake Improvement Association was instrumental in having the earlier one moved off the beach, behind this one on Worthington Avenue, which is now a private home. (Postcard, collection of Richard Napolitan.)

This snapshot of a boy on a bicycle passing a horse-drawn cart shows the open spaces of the north end of Spring Lake along Prospect Avenue in the early days of the century. (Courtesy of Dr. C. Wrege.)

This home with an enviable view to the ocean dates from the 1880s and was the design of Philadelphia architects George Ward and William Hewitt for Rev. Thomas A. Willson. The original Shingle style house was subsequently remodeled and its porches enclosed in this view, when it was apparently used as a convalescent home. In 1911, it became the home of Robert A. Chesebrough, inventor of Vaseline petroleum jelly, who remodeled it in a Neo Classical style and continued to call it Seacroft. The house was eventually demolished. (Collection of Richard Napolitan.)

The Spring Lake Borough Improvement Association, an organization of business and property owners as well as summer cottagers, created a lasting gift to the borough by donating the ornamental portal at the northern boundary of Ocean Avenue, *c.* 1920. The arched, brick structures, capped with cast stone finials and "Spring Lake" inscribed in classical lettering, originally featured bronze pendant lights. The gateway (which never had "gates") was built by private subscription at a cost of over $5,700. The builder Horace H. Moore was both the contractor and a contributor. (Collection of Dick Napolitan.)

This swan was an early descendant of the first swans donated in 1912. (Courtesy of Jennie Lee Aitkenhead.) The author welcomes responses from readers, including additional material and reminiscences. Please contact the author at the following: Patricia F. Colrick, P.O. 160, Spring Lake, New Jersey 07762.